The Art of
COMMUNICATION

Whether you're in the office or at a dinner party, nothing is more important than saying the most appropriate thing in the best possible way. Now this powerful communication tool gives you specific success phrases that will help you:

BREAK THE ICE

When meeting someone for the first time,
don't be afraid to ask:
"Am I pronouncing your name correctly?"

BE UP!

If someone asks you how you are, try "Splendid!"
It makes a great impression!

GET ALONG

Saying "we" instead of "I" will bring your co-workers
over to your side—even in a difficult situation.

BE HELPFUL

"Please feel free to discuss this matter with me
at any time, including now" is a great way
to let someone know you care.

BE ASSERTIVE

You have the right to say
"This is unsatisfactory!" when someone
is inconsiderate to you.

With dozens of phrases to choose from in any real-life situation, THE RIGHT WORDS is the only compendium available that actually puts hundreds of communication choices at your fingertips—and helps you find the right ones for you.

The Art of
COMMUNICATION

THE
RIGHT
WORDS

THE 350 BEST THINGS
TO SAY TO GET
ALONG WITH PEOPLE

Irwin M. Berent and
Rod L. Evans

WARNER BOOKS

A Time Warner Company

WARNER BOOKS EDITION

Cover design by Diane Luger

Warner Books, Inc.
1271 Avenue of the Americas
New York, N.Y. 10020

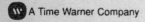 A Time Warner Company

Printed in the United States of America

First Printing: December, 1992

10 9 8 7 6 5 4 3 2 1

Contents

Introduction

This book contains the most effective phrases and sentences in the English language. By using them habitually, you will project the image of a powerful speaker and dynamic conversationalist. What's more, using these expressions can help you to be calmer and friendlier, as well as more honest, assertive, and considerate.

Although this book contains one chapter written specifically for getting along with co-workers, bosses, and employees (chapter 4) and another chapter specifically for getting things done at work, virtually every Success Phrase in this book will assist you in getting along with everyone with whom you come in contact. The chapter on handling criticism (chapter 7), for example, contains Success Phrases that can be applied effectively with virtually anyone who criticizes you.

Why Use Success Phrases?

Success Phrases help people get along with others, whether they are friends, family members, co-workers, supervisors, or adversaries. When you effectively use these phrases you'll tend to get what you want from others: respect, friendship, support, and cooperation. And since respect, friendship, support, and cooperation are usually necessary for happiness, Success Phrases can play an important role in determining the quality of your life.

Commonly, when you treat people well, they will treat you well. When you treat people as equals, they generally will treat you as an equal. And since one of the principal ways in which you express your respect and regard for people is through the use of language, you have reason to master techniques for effective speech.

When you use Success Phrases, you show respect for others as well as for yourself; you get what you want and help others at the same time; you enhance others' self-esteem as you enhance your own.

Make Friends . . . and Keep Friends!

Perhaps the quickest way to lose your friends is to take them for granted. A simple "please" and "thank you" can go a long way toward keeping a friendship alive. Further, politeness will impress strangers and attract them to you. Especially today, those who show courtesy and tact are a prized few and stand out in any crowd.

Indeed, when you habitually use Success Phrases, you'll find that it's easy to maintain friendships and difficult to make enemies. For it will be nearly impossible for people to stay angry with you—and for you to stay angry with them.

Getting the Most out of Success Phrases

In this book, you'll usually be given several expressions to accomplish each communication goal. So that you can choose the one that is most appropriate for your circumstance. If you feel that some of the expressions "just don't sound like me," ignore them and use the one that feels best. If you find none with which you feel comfortable, feel free to alter any of them or to write your own expressions that embody the same principle.

Using some of these expressions may come naturally to you; using others may take some practice. Try to resist thinking that a certain expression "goes without saying." Kind words and honest words are almost always appropriate; and assertive words often are necessary. If you find some expressions particularly difficult to use, try telling your conversational partner: "This phrase is in a book I'm reading, and I'd like to try it out on you."

With practice, these powerful expressions will become second nature to you.

/

Being a Friend

We sometimes make the mistake of assuming that our friends, co-workers, and companions "just know" how much we respect them, admire their accomplishments, and appreciate their kindness. Therefore, we assume that we needn't express our feelings and attitudes to them verbally.

This assumption is unjustified. First, it takes for granted the mistaken belief that people will always understand our feelings and attitudes, when in fact even our closest friends, to whom we reveal confidences, can misunderstand us.

Second, this assumption ignores a fact about human nature: People deeply appreciate signs of caring, including those expressed in language.

Third, and finally, this assumption is unwise and shortsighted because, in effect, it measures the importance of people according to how useful they appear to our immediate interests. That standard of measurement violates the ethical injunction to treat others as we ourselves would like to be treated. In addition, it is unacceptable even from a self-interested point of view, from which we can see that it is foolish to think that showing little regard for people we encounter won't ultimately hurt us, either by alienating people or by lowering our self-esteem. We can also admit that we often don't know who will eventually be able to help us. For example, often people who we don't think can help us in our careers have contacts with people who can.

In short, it is in our self-interest to be the sort of people who are loyal and reliable. Such people try to treat others as they themselves want to be treated, and they *don't* constantly try to determine which people are important and which are "unimportant."

The upshot, then, is that we'd be both wise and prudent to treat people well and to express our good feelings for them frequently and in plain language.

In This Section

The expressions in this section are designed to reveal your willingness to cooperate with others, to help them get what they want, and to show your appreciation for their help and accomplishments.

Where friendship and charity are concerned, strive to be cooperative, deliberate, prompt, and reliable. Be a doer, not an avoider.

"Yes."
"I will . . ."
"I'm flexible."
"I'll do it right away."
"I promise."
"I'll accept full responsibility."
"I accept responsibility for . . ."

Strive to be an enthusiastic supporter, not a grouch.

"I'm eager to . . ."
"Let's give it a try."
"It's worth a try."
"That might work."
"That's something to consider."
"That's an interesting idea."
"You have a good idea; don't give up on it.
   Look at it from other angles. There's *always* at
   least one answer."
"Wow!"
"Great!"
"Fantastic!"
"Nice job!"

Express your admiration, loyalty, and respect for your
friends and associates.

"I admire you."
"I value your opinion."
"I listen to what you say."
"I believe you."

"I believe in you."

"I trust you."

"I'm impressed with your . . ."

"I respect you."

"I appreciate your . . ."

"I look up to you."

"I applaud [or 'commend'] your . . ."

"I'll stand up for you."

"I'll let others know about your . . ."

"I'll recommend your . . ."

"You're an inspiration."

"Your . . . has inspired [or 'influenced'] me."

"I'm proud of you."

"I'm proud that you're my friend."

"I've learned a lot from you."

"I wish I had your . . ."

"I wish I could . . . as well as you."

"You're wonderful!"

"You're terrific!"

Stand up for your friends by defending them against anyone who speaks abusively about them. Your friends will appreciate your support, and others will know that you are loyal to your friends.

"I know [name of friend] well enough to know that your remarks are unfair; he's one of the most considerate people I know."

"I don't appreciate your criticizing my friends, especially behind their backs."

"Please try to see the matter from her point of

view; she has reasons for feeling that way
about it.''

Avoid listening to rumors about others, which can be
destructive to everyone.

"I make it a practice to avoid hearing rumors,
which are often distorted.''
"I'm sorry, but I'm not interested in other
people's personal lives.''
"Just as I would refuse to hear rumors about
you, so I am refusing to hear rumors about
him.''
"She is a friend of mine, and I don't wish to
listen to gossip about her.''
"I prefer that people not spread rumors about
me, so I make it a practice to avoid listening
to rumors about others, which are often
inaccurate and none of my business.''

Delight in the accomplishments of others.

"I'm glad that things have gone so well for
you.''
"I deeply enjoy hearing about your successes.''
"I admire your accomplishment.''
"Please let me know about any further good
news.''

Notice the kind things that people do for you. Thank
them for even the smallest acts of kindness. You can
even thank them just for being important to you.

"Thanks for your help."
"That means a lot to me."
"I'm glad you did that."
"I enjoyed your . . ."
"I appreciate your thinking of me."
"I can really use this."
"I'll treasure this."
"I appreciate this."
"I love you."
"That is very kind of you."
"It was so nice of you to . . ."
"I've been thinking about you."
"I'm glad to see you."
"I've missed you."
"I like the way you think."
"Your friendship means a lot to me."
"You've made my day."
"This is a pleasant surprise."
"I always enjoy talking to you."
"I like the way I feel when I'm with you."

Acknowledge compliments graciously. Ignoring or denying compliments may appear to impugn the complimenter's judgment.

"Thanks, you're very kind to say that."
"I'm glad you enjoyed it."
"I'm pleased you think so."
"Thank you for noticing."
"Thanks, I appreciate that."

"Thanks, that means a lot to me."
"I like to hear that."

Show that you notice specific attributes in your friends by giving "You . . ." compliments. Using "you" is more personal and direct than using "that" (e.g., "That's a good idea," versus, "You have good ideas," or, "That's a pretty dress," versus, "You have great taste in clothes").

"You* do good work."
"You try hard."
"You're very dedicated to . . ."
"You really love your . . ."
"You're a loyal friend."
"You certainly know a lot about . . ."
"You're very good at . . ."
"You're always willing to help."
"You keep your cool."
"You're a fair man/woman."
"You make people feel important."
"You're always the first to admit when you're
    wrong."
"You're always open to new ideas."
"You're a good teacher because you . . ."
"You're a good listener because you . . ."
"You're a hard worker."
"You look nice [or 'pretty' or 'handsome']."

*Note that prefacing "you" with the person's name is also extremely effective.

Compliment people, even when you feel tempted to criticize them. Compliments usually motivate people better than do criticisms.

"You're doing a lot better at . . ."
"I see improvement in your . . ."
"You're getting better at . . ."
"You tried, and you did well at . . ."
"It's so nice when you . . ."
"I love the way you . . ."
"That was an excellent attempt."
"You showed great restraint to hold out for as long as you did before you gave in this time."
"That's the best you've ever done that."
"Considering the difficulty, you're doing very well at . . ."

Commend people for accomplishing difficult emotional tasks, such as accepting criticism, apologizing, and being assertive.

"It took a lot of courage for you to . . ."
"I know that was difficult for you to do; I appreciate your courage."
"You deserve to be commended for admitting the mistake."

Accept your friends' differences, and allow them to disagree with you without making them feel as if there is something wrong with them.

"It's okay with me that you like that [TV program/type of music], even though I have a different preference."

"I can accept that your tastes are at times different from mine."

"I have no problems with your [political/ religious] opinions; we come from different backgrounds, so differences of opinion can be expected."

"Please feel free to differ with me on this matter."

Assure your friends—especially when they disagree with you—that you are tolerant of diversity.

"I realize that people have a right to be individuals."

"I expect people to act according to their own experiences and not according to my values."

"As the cliché goes, differences of opinion make horse races."

"Different strokes for different folks."

"I realize that nothing varies as much as taste."

"I can easily live with people who are different from me."

Show your respect for others, and don't ask people to justify their actions to you. When people begin offering explanations for their bad behavior or mistakes, show them that you trust their motives and don't want to judge them.

"Please don't explain—I trust you and forgive you."

"You don't have to tell me why you did it; I just want you to know how I feel about it."

"I'm not judging your actions; your reasons are your own, and I'm sure you didn't mean to do it."

"I appreciate your apology—no explanations are necessary."

Show that you care about others by confiding in them.

"You're the first [or 'only'] person I've told this to."*

Help make your friends feel willing to come to you whenever they feel the need to talk to someone.

"Because I care about you, I want you to know that you can tell me whatever is on your mind in strictest confidence."

"Please feel free to confide in me; I don't judge friends—I support them."

"You need to know that you can trust me."

"I listen to friends with understanding, not judgment.

Show that you respect others' abilities by occasionally asking for their help or advice, even when you might be able to do without it.

*Of course, you'll want to say this only if it is true.

"Could you help me?"
"Since I believe that you are especially capable,
    I'd appreciate your helping me."
"Could you give me a hand with this?"
"I could really use your advice."

Show a willingness to work together and share with others.

"This is my treat."
"Here, take [or 'use'] mine."
"You can have mine."
"Let's work together on this."

Ask your friends for their permission—even when you know the answer will be "yes."

"Will it be okay if I . . . ?"
"Do you have any problems with my [doing
    something]?"
"Do you agree with this decision?"
"May I . . . ?"
"Am I correct in assuming that you . . . ?"

Show that you care about others by involving them in your activities.

"Would you like to go with me to . . . ?"
"I'd be happy to have you come along."
"I'd like you to accompany me."
"I'd enjoy your company."

Try to find out what others prefer.

"What would you like me to do?"
"Where do you want to go?"
"What's your preference?"
"What would you like to do?"
"How would you prefer to handle this?"

Include those whom you want to feel a part of some activity or accomplishment by often using "we" and "our" when you speak (instead of speaking only of what "I" did or of "my" such and such).

"We've worked hard on this."
"We came up with some good ideas."
"Our plan [or 'goal'] is to . . ."
"This is our project."

Make it easy for your friends to meet one another by making sure you introduce them.

"[Name], do you know [name]?"
"[Name], have you met my friend [name]?"
"[Name], I'd like you to meet [name]."

2

Meeting People and Being a Good Conversationalist

There is an art to meeting people and engaging them in productive conversation. Although meeting people and developing new friendships are important to enjoying life, many people lack the skills necessary to carry on enjoyable conversations. The good news is that you can improve your conversations by learning and using language that is effective at breaking down social barriers and developing rapport.

In This Section

Since the first step in meeting people is to begin conversation, in this section you'll learn language that is effective for introducing yourself and getting others' attention.

You will learn also how to keep conversations going with techniques for expressing enthusiasm for your conversational partner's point of view and for asking stimulating questions. In short, you'll learn how to focus much of the conversation on your partner, who will appreciate your interest.

Meet people just by introducing yourself.

"Hi [or 'hello'], my name is* . . . What's yours?"

Value people's names. Since people feel more important and appreciated when you use their names, pay attention to their names when you first meet them, and then use their names throughout the conversation. There are a number of ways that you can remember the names (including simply repeating them).

"Could you spell that?"
"Could you repeat that?"
"What's the origin of that name?"
"Am I pronouncing your name correctly?"

Vary your greetings. Trite or overused greetings often lack enthusiasm and sincerity.

"Excellent morning, isn't it?" [instead of "Good morning."]

*You can mention just your first name, or you can include your last name if you want to know theirs.

"I hope everything is going well for you."
   [instead of "How are you?"]

Personalize your greetings to people you've met previously.

"Good to see you, [name]; how's your [project/
   plan/work] coming along?"
"Glad you're here, [name]; how's your [family/
   son/daughter/husband/wife]?"
"Hello, [name]; I was happy to hear about
   your . . ."

Greet friends and associates with enthusiasm and warmth.

"I'm glad to see you!"
"I'm happy you're here!"
"Thanks for coming."
"Now that you're here, I know I'm going to be
   in a good mood."

Respond to people's greetings with a variety of positive remarks. When others ask, "How are you," try, for example, saying something besides simply, "Okay," or, "Pretty good."

"Splendid!"
"Couldn't be better!"
"Delighted!"

In your conversations, show enthusiasm and appreciation for what the other says. These responses boost people's confidence and encourage them to speak more. They also help keep conversations going when you can't think of anything to say.

"That's interesting. I didn't know that."
"Interesting! Tell me more about it."
"I've never heard that before. That's interesting."
"I agree."
"I had never thought of that."
"I'd never heard it put that way."
"I'd never heard it put so clearly."
"You have a good point."

Listen for and acknowledge the good in what people tell you.

"That sounds fantastic."
"You must have really enjoyed that."
"You must be very proud."
"That's wonderful!"
"Wow!"

In your conversations, find out about the other person; constantly use "you" in your questions. You won't have to worry about what to say because you'll have ample questions to ask, and your conversations won't be cluttered with talk solely about yourself ("I," "me," "my"). Further, your conversational partners will be pleased that you're interested in them.

>"Where are you from?"
>"Are you enjoying the area?"
>"What do you do?"
>"How long have you been in the business?"
>"What do you like to do when you're not working?"
>"How are you enjoying the [party/convention/class/flight]?"
>"What do you think about . . . ?"
>"How did you happen to . . . ?"
>"How did you feel when . . . ?"
>"What is most interesting to you about your work?"

In your conversations, encourage others to express their opinions.

>"In your opinion, what . . . ?"
>"What's your opinion?"
>"What do you think?"
>"Do you have a different opinion?"

If people cite inaccurate statistics, generally avoid correcting them. However, if you feel that it is important that they be made aware of the facts, correct them—but do so *gently*. You do not want to give your conversational partners the impression that you're a know-it-all or that you're hard to get along with. You also do not want to risk losing track of what the people are saying or to appear that you are not listening to their whole message.

"I think you may be mistaken about that exact figure."

"I believe that the actual figure is about . . . , but that's really a minor difference."

"That's very close, although I think the fact is that . . ."

"You're practically right on the money; the only thing that is probably not quite correct is your statement that . . ."

"What you are saying is correct with only one exception, and that is . . ."

"It's my understanding that . . ."

Try always to be positive about others' remarks, even if you disagree with them. If you have doubts about the value of some belief or plan, and you feel that expressing approval would be inappropriate, ask sincere questions that will help to draw out other points of view. Such questions will almost always be more effective and productive than such offensive statements as, "That's ridiculous!" or, "That's a screwy belief," or, "Where did you get that crazy notion?"

"Do you think there might be any evidence against your belief?"

"Do you think some people might reject your
    suggested [reform/idea/plan]?"
"What led you to that conclusion?"

Be well read and you'll almost never be at a loss for
something to say in a conversation.

"Today, I read . . ."
"Your remark is echoed by . . . , whose column
    [or 'book' or 'article'] developed a similar line
    of argument."

Have some thought-provoking questions in the ready
for whenever a conversation needs rejuvenating.

"Do you know how to spell . . . ?"
"Do you know the origin of the phrase . . . ?"
"Do you know what . . . means?"
"How many words can you think of that end
    in . . . ?"
"Name as many kinds of . . . as you can think
    of."
"What would you do if you won one million
    dollars?"
"What would you do if you had only one day [or
    'one month'] to live?"
"Where would you go if you were invisible?"
"What five books would you want on a deserted
    island?"

"If you could do any kind of work you wanted,
  what would it be?"

"If you could live your life over, how would you
  make it different?"

"If you could be any person you know or have
  read about, in any period of history, who
  would it be?"

"If you won a free ticket to travel anywhere,
  where would you go?"

Whenever your listeners appear confused by what you
say, take responsibility for the confusion by politely
asking in what ways you may clarify your ideas. If
you think their confusion is based on their indifference
or inattention, don't give up, but repeat yourself, perhaps using a slightly louder voice.

"Am I making myself clear?"

"Would you like me to give you an example?"

"Could you tell me what, if anything, you find
  confusing?"

"If that's not immediately clear, don't feel bad;
  it can be complicated."

Before your conversation ends, express your pleasure
at having spoken with the other person.

"You've made me think."

"I really enjoyed our conversation."

"I really enjoyed talking to you."

Vary your closings, trying your best to leave others with a smile on your face—and on theirs.

> "Good luck to you!" [instead of 'Take it easy.']
> "Best wishes for an outstanding day!" [instead of 'Have a good one' or—God forbid!—'Have a nice day.']

3

Being Helpful

One of the most effective ways to get along with people and to develop rich, lasting friendships is to express an interest in their lives and a concern for them. While most of us would help our friends when they need help, we sometimes don't verbalize our concern and our readiness to help. Yet, such words can be a source of great comfort and strength to people.

In This Section

In this section you'll learn to use language that can bring you closer to those you care about by not only expressing your willingness to help, but also reassuring them that they have the power to overcome obstacles and worries. Accordingly, you'll learn to defuse people's worries, boost their self-confidence, and help them set goals. In short, you will learn language that will help you inspire people, enabling them to fulfill their potentials. By helping people help themselves, you can gain satisfaction and enrich your friendships.

Show that you'll be there for your friends.

"I care."
"Is something bothering you? Would you like to talk about it?"
"Please feel free to discuss this matter at any time, including now."
"I'm available whenever you need me, including now."
"You can count on me."

Show a willingness to give your time to help others.

"I have time to . . ."
"I'll be glad to help."
"How may I help you?"
"Is there anything I can do?"
"What do you want me to do?"
"Don't worry about me—I'm glad to help."
"No problem; I'm eager to help."

Make your offers of help easy for others to accept.

"I won't take no for an answer."
"What help do you need from me?"

"What would you like me to do right now?"
"I want to help you; please tell me what I can do."
*"When can I help you do this?"

Help lead people to identifying and seeking solutions to obvious personal problems.†

"What do you think is the main source of the problem?"
"What factors have contributed to the problem?"
"How have I contributed to the situation?"
"What ideas do you have for solving the problem?"
"What are you going to do to take action?"
"What needs to happen—and when?"
"What help will you need?"
"What will you need from me?"
"Should anyone else be told or involved?"
"Do you think that professional counseling would help?"
"When would you like to talk again?"

When people have something important or emotional to tell you, first establish eye contact, then let them

---

*By asking "*when*" you "can" help rather than whether you "may" help, you've taken it for granted that you'll be helping and therefore have made it more probable that your offer will be accepted.
†Naturally, you must be the ultimate judge of whether the person would be responsive to your help. Tact and good judgment are required.

know that they have your undivided attention—and *give* them your undivided attention.

"You have my undivided attention."
"I promise that I'll listen carefully and not interrupt."
"I'm going to forget about doing that [the activity that you were engaged in] and pay attention only to what you want to tell me."

When your friends tell you their problems, show them that you understand how they feel.

"I'm disappointed that things didn't work out as you had hoped."
"I want to be sure I understand you; what I hear you saying is . . ."
"I can relate to . . ."
"You feel that . . ."
"I see what you mean."
"I'd feel the same way if I were in your shoes."

When people express vulnerable emotions, such as anxiety and apprehension, try to show empathy by relating their feelings and situations to your experience. (Follow this advice only if you can *sincerely* discuss similar feelings and experiences.)

"Believe me, I know what it's like to have that happen; a few years ago . . ."

"I can appreciate how you feel because I've been
in similar situations."

Help defuse people's worries by getting them to consider realistically the implications of their fears.

"What's the worst that could happen?"
"What's the probability that your worst fears
would be realized?"
"Can you possibly see yourself as saying 'so
what?' to the prospect that your worst fear
could happen?"

Remind troubled people of their blessings, accomplishments, and goals.

"When I become depressed, I think of all the
things for which I'm grateful; you're also
blessed with many gifts, including [high
intelligence/good health . . .]."
"You're forgetting that you have dealt with these
kinds of problems before with great success."
"You've overlooked the goals in which you are
succeeding; for example, . . ."

Help people by explaining how *they* are usually the
principal authors of their emotions and therefore have
the power to redirect those emotions.

"Although he did something to you that you
dislike, *you* can decide whether you're going
to let that upset you."

"There's no law that says that what insensitive
people do or say to others must be taken
seriously."

"That insensitive person didn't anger you; you
angered yourself by unrealistically believing
that all people *must* behave the way you and I
would like them to."

"Her behavior wouldn't have affected you if you
had understood it as a product of an insecure
person [or 'a distraught person' or 'a jealous
person' or 'a person who did not know
better']."

Reassure people when they doubt their abilities or fear
the future.

"I know you can . . ."

"I know you'll do fine."

"I have total confidence in your ability."

Help boost people's self-confidence by challenging
any of their self-depreciating "I know" assumptions
(e.g., "I know I'm going to fail," or "I know they
won't like me").

"How do you know?"

"Are you a mind reader?"

"Can you foretell the future?"

Discourage others' self-depreciating statements, such
as, "I'm no good at this," "I've really been a fool,"
and "Boy, I'm so stupid."

"I've made the same kind of mistake before."

"Don't label yourself a [self-depreciating label]
just because on this one occasion you did
that."

"You're not a [self-depreciating label]; it's
human to be imperfect."

"You're being too hard on yourself."

"Don't be so quick to put yourself down; usually
you [description of a related accomplishment
of the person]."

Help people eliminate their beliefs that they "must,"
"must not," "should," "should not," "have to," or
"can't" do certain things—in other words, that they
lack control over their lives—by encouraging them
to think about what would happen if they did have
control.

"What if you didn't assume that?"

"What would happen if you were able to do that
[or "if you chose not to do that"]?"

"How would you act if you didn't accept that
rule?"

Help people set major goals.

"If you believed that success were inevitable,
what concrete steps would you take?"

"If you believed that failure were impossible,
what concrete steps would you take?"

"What would have to happen for you to feel really fulfilled?"

"What do you want?"

"How do you want to change things?"

Help people develop their ideas by asking them questions that inspire their creativity.

"If you were a magician, or an omnipotent god, in what ways could you change this idea?"

"What would happen if you combined this with something completely unrelated to it?"

"How would someone else—say, a mail carrier, a carpenter, a police officer, or an artist—tend to view this idea and want to change it?"

"Can you do something silly with your idea, say, turn it upside down to see what ideas that reversal might generate?"

4

Getting Along with Co-Workers, Bosses, and Employees

Many people spend at least forty hours a week working with people with whom they don't get along. Such people feel drained from having to work with others whose habits, including verbal habits, they find disagreeable. Fortunately, you can improve your relationships with fellow workers as well as supervisors by habitually using language that promotes harmony rather than discord.

If you habitually use language that builds people up rather than tears them down and that reflects a concern for your job, co-workers, and supervisors, your work will be both more enjoyable and more productive. What's more, you may even find that your self-esteem improves because of your regularly inspiring others.

In This Section

In this section you'll learn to make suggestions to, and express disagreements with, supervisors and associates, accept and give criticism, obey and issue directives and praise co-workers and supervisors. Try to avoid language that makes your boss or supervisor feel like a dictator.

"What other duties [instead of "demands"] do
   you have for me?"
"Do you have any further tasks [instead of
   "orders"]?"
"What other guidelines [instead of "laws" or
   "rules"] do you want me to work under?"

When your boss or supervisor does something you like, cheerfully tell him or her how much you appreciate it.

"I want to thank you for adding fifteen minutes
   to the lunch break; we workers really
   appreciate it."
"I'm glad to tell you how happy I am with the
   raise—thanks!"
"The other workers and I are happy with your
   show of concern."

When praising a supervisor, co-worker, or employee, be specific.

"I really appreciate your letting me go home early because of my dinner party." [Instead of simply, "You're a nice supervisor."]

"I want you to know that I value your advice about how to learn those new procedures." [Instead of simply, "You've been helpful."]

"I deeply appreciate your putting in those extra hours to complete your current assignment." [Instead of simply, "You're a good worker."]

Before interrupting subordinates to give them additional directives, preface your remarks with expressions that reflect good manners.

"Excuse me . . ."

"Pardon me . . ."

"Will you please . . . ?"

"When you have the time, I'd appreciate . . ."

"This will *really* be a help to me: could you . . . ?"

Be quick to defend not only co-workers but also supervisors against unfair criticism.

"Please understand that our supervisor is under enormous pressure and that his rudeness stems from stress, not malice."

"I wanted our boss to help us [on this project] as much as you did, but we need to remember that we aren't the only people he has to supervise."

Seek frequent evaluations from those whom you are managing. That practice shows that you care about both accomplishing quality work and pleasing your co-workers.

"How well am I directing this project?"

"How do you think it could be better?"

"How do you feel about what's being accomplished, and what do you feel still needs to be done?"

"One of my goals was to . . . ; how am I doing?"

"How has this project hindered you?"

"What could I do in the future to help prevent or solve some of these problems?"

When workers express their problems, show that you are listening and sympathetic by paraphrasing and by drawing conclusions from their statements.

"I understand, from what you've said, that when the other workers criticize your performance, you feel embarrassed and frustrated."

"You're saying, in effect, that you've been assigned too many tasks to perform them well."

"Would I be right in saying that you're unhappy with your supervisor's evaluation of your performance?"

If a subordinate has complaints or difficulties, don't dismiss the problems as part of the job or as trivial; instead, express your concern for the subordinate's point of view.

> "Can you explain specifically why you're having trouble?"
> "How can we get the job done *and* remove this problem?"
> "Since I value your opinion, I'd like to know whether you can think of a more effective way to accomplish your duties that would be acceptable to both of us?"

Help those who have carried out assignments for you to examine their performance and always to strive for improvement. This practice shows that you are concerned both with having the assignment done well and with their learning and growing from the experience. (Remember, however, that you will always want to offer compliments and praise for whatever you can find that is commendable in their performance.)

> "What did you find most instructive about this assignment?"
> "What, if anything, would you want to do differently next time?"
> "What difficulties did you have?"
> "How could you have anticipated problems sooner?"

"Should you have asked for more help (or less
   help)?"
"Did you use all the resources available to you?"
"Were you happy with your increased
   responsibilities?"

When your supervisor criticizes your performance,
avoid becoming defensive, but ask for details, especially about what you might have done differently.

"You say that I'm rude to customers; could you
   please be a bit more specific?"
"Since I want to do a good job and wrongly
   thought that I had met your standards, I'd
   appreciate it if you could explain how I might
   improve my performance."

When your supervisor or subordinates criticize your
performance, try to find something with which you
can express agreement.

"I appreciate your concern, since I suppose I do
   sometimes overreact to stress by calling
   demanding customers 'dictators.' "
"You're right that I sometimes . . . In my
   defense, though, I do want to point out that
   . . ."

When you see a problem that your fellow workers are
creating, first ask yourself whether it's fair to mention
the problem. You might also want to consider whether

they will dislike your mentioning it. If you feel that the problem is still worth mentioning, mention it without casting blame.

> "I'm sure that you didn't mean to . . ."
> "I think that you didn't realize that . . ."
> "This is a mistake anyone could make."

Before suggesting a new approach to replace one that you believe is flawed, be sure to preface your suggestion with words that reflect your conscientiousness and concern for the company.

> "I'm making the following suggestion not to condemn our current methods but to try to improve our approach—to make a good approach even better."
> "While our current procedures are effective, I believe that the approach I'm about to suggest could be even *more* effective than those, for if we . . . , then we'd be able to . . ."

Avoid directly criticizing people for failing, and try instead to compliment them for any improvement whatsoever.

> "This latest draft of your magazine article skillfully presents all sides of the issue and is especially well researched, so now you need only add a few conclusions, and you'll come close to perfection." [Instead of, "Your article

is deficient because you've omitted some
conclusions.'']

"I like the way you're getting the perimeter of
the store cleaned now, and if you'll use
roughly that same method to clean up the
interior floors, you'll have done an
extraordinary job.'' [Instead of, ''These floors
are still a mess!'']

If you feel you must criticize, make sure that you
criticize the *actions* and not the people who perform
them.

"Next time it might be helpful to read the
instructions carefully before operating the
machine.'' [Instead of, ''You're an
incompetent employee.'']

"In the future it might be useful to exercise more
authority over your employees.'' [Instead of,
''You're a weak manager.'']

"Let's try to make an effort to be more careful
next time.'' [Instead of, ''You're a real
bungler.'']

When you must criticize people who you think may
be particularly sensitive, make it quite clear that you
are not disapproving of *them* but only of what they are
doing.

"Please realize that there is nothing wrong with
you; rather, it is simply that we've found that

our new technique usually works better than
the one you've been using.''
"Please note that when I ask you to spend more
time with techniques I'm not casting blame; I
simply want each employee to be as efficient
as possible.''

When people repeatedly fail to discharge their responsibilities properly, adopt a posture of "creative stern-
ness,'' in which you reprimand people for their actions
but (as usual) don't attack them personally.

"I've asked you at least three times to perform
that task, and each time you promised to do it
immediately; yet you haven't even begun—can
you tell me what the problem is?''
"I don't enjoy riding people, but we all have
responsibilities, and many people depend on
us.''

Before expressing particularly serious suggestions or
complaints, try to discuss specific examples without
being negative about current procedures.

"There may be a way of changing our procedures
to save money.''
"Doing it another way may help us save work.''
"The last four times that we asked everyone to
try to close just one more sale, we doubled our
sales; so I think it would be a good idea once

again to ask everyone to go for one more
sale.''

If you have reservations about someone's suggestion,
try to be as tactful as possible, concentrating princi-
pally on what's *right* about the suggestion.

"Your suggestion has merits—in fact, we tried
it before with some success—so the *only*
reason we'd prefer to avoid that approach now
is . . .''
"I appreciate your suggestion, and my only
concern is that if we follow it, we'll run into
the following obstacle: . . . If you can think of
a way around that obstacle, I'm all ears.''

If your supervisor asks your opinion of a plan, and
you think the plan is flawed, resist the temptation to
condemn the plan, but explain how it might be made
more effective.

"I like your idea of giving our customers a gift
on Christmas, and while a pencil and pen set is
a good idea, perhaps a turkey might be even
more appreciated.''
"That's an interesting idea, and I think that with
the exception of . . .—which we might want
to change to : . .—it will work out great.''

If you are uncertain exactly what your boss or supervisor wants you to do on some occasion, don't assume

that you know; instead, politely explain that you'd like more details.

> "Please give me some more details about the task you've assigned; I think I might not have fully understood you."
> "Please give me some more information about what you want me to do, because I'm not quite certain about the details."
> "When you explained my duties, I was unsure whether my responsibility extended to doing . . . ; could you elaborate on that?"
> "Am I correct in assuming that you want me to . . . ?"

In business, try to use more-formal expressions.

> "Hello." [not "Hi"]
> "Yes." [not "Yeah"]
> "Surely." [not "Sure"]
> "Will you please wait?" [not "Wait a sec" or "Hold on"]

When waiting on customers or screening phone calls, try to avoid asking, "What do you want?"; instead, use more-polite expressions.

> "May I help you?"
> "What can I do for you today?"
> "May I be of service?"

5

Giving Advice
and Criticism

We often think that people "should be able to take a little constructive criticism." Sometimes we even feel that criticism *should* hurt, at least a little. Admittedly, giving advice and criticism that won't hurt people's feelings is difficult; nonetheless, there *are*, happily, techniques for giving advice and criticism that are both productive and sensitive.

Consider first that praise is usually more effective than criticism; thus, it is wise to try to avoid criticism and to make it as positive as possible when you must use it.

You'll find that you'll be able to make your criticism more positive by trying to imagine yourself in the place of the person you're criticizing. You may find it difficult to identify with someone who did something of which you disapprove, but you need to realize that we are all imperfect and that we can improve *ourselves* most effectively when people sensitively try to correct our conduct and do not belittle us.

Most of us profit more from being corrected by those who speak from concern than by those who speak from power and authority. For that reason, it is important for you to avoid putting people down by making them feel inadequate. Note also that criticism that makes people feel anxious, fearful, and incompetent is likely to backfire, since people who are plagued by fear and self-doubts are less likely to function effectively.

In This Section

In this section you'll learn how to apply the principles behind the art of giving advice and criticism. Those principles are easy to understand: First, mention something positive about the person's performance before you criticize it. Second, avoid emotional language that goes beyond describing what the person has done and demands a justification for the act. Third, avoid language that attacks people rather than corrects their conduct. Fourth, and finally, avoid authoritarian and threatening language, (as in, ''You *must* do what I demand, or you'll be looking for another job''), by which people are intimidated. Before you give criticism or advice to someone, give the person a compliment or show that you appreciate the person's point of view or feelings. Further, avoid using ''but'' or ''however'' when you start the criticism. ''But'' and "however" suggest opposition, whereas a word such as "and" suggests support.

"I appreciate the intensity of your feelings about this, and [not "but"] I think if you were to hear my side of it you might feel differently."

"I can understand your reasons, and I think my reasons for doing it differently are also understandable."

"I can understand why you would have done that. You might also want to consider that . . ."

"I can understand how you might feel . . ."

"I respect your thinking, and I think you can also see why I might think differently."

"I agree with much of what you're saying, and the only concern I have is . . ."

"That's true, and here's something else that's true."

"That's an interesting idea, and here's another way to think about it."

When you're tempted to criticize people for something they did, calmly ask them to *describe* their actions. That response vents your concern or anger and keeps you from demanding that they justify their actions to you (which is what we do when we ask "Why did you do that?").

"How did you do that?"

"What did you do?"

When giving criticism, focus on people's future successes, not their past failures.

"The next time, I'd like you to . . ." [instead of, "Don't blow it like you did *last* time!"]

When giving criticism or advice, avoid using words that sound exceedingly negative or as if you are making a moral judgment (as in "You are wrong").

"You may be incorrect."
"That action may be inappropriate."
"Your contention may be erroneous [or "mistaken" or "inaccurate"]."
"That decision may be inadvisable."
"That response may be questionable."

In your criticism, focus primarily on correcting the problem or mistake rather than on condemning it. Use language that is solution-oriented, not problem-oriented.

"I don't want you to feel guilty about what you did; rather, I want you to consider some concrete ways to improve your performance in the future."
"We can't change what you did, but we can adopt methods for making sure that the same kind of thing doesn't occur again."
"You're human and so made a mistake; the main

concern now is with what we are going to do
to prevent it from happening again.''

When criticizing someone's actions, rather than condemning the person, try to make the person see his
mistake by asking questions to persuade him to realize
and admit the mistake.

"How do you think he felt when you did that to
him?''
"What do you think were the consequences of
your doing that?''

Keep advice, criticisms, and other forms of informa-
tion-giving precise by acknowledging the source of
your "knowledge." For what you may claim "they
say" or "is absolutely true" or "everyone knows" or
"common sense tells you" is often not true and may
be merely what you *think* is true or what works for
you.

"This is based on . . .''
"I've heard several people say that . . .''
"A number of experts have said that . . .''
"This is just a pet peeve of mine. Would you
mind . . . ?''
"My personal opinion is . . .''
"It's my understanding that . . .''
"I've always assumed that . . .''
"In my personal experience, I have found
that . . .''

"It seems to me . . ."
"I think . . ."
"I believe . . ."
"This is just my opinion."

When offering advice, speak about what *you* would do or how you have handled similar problems instead of what the person you're advising "should" or "must" do. Advice is best received when it doesn't dictate what someone should do.

"*I* would . . ."
"This has worked well for me: . . ."
"When . . . has happened to me, I have often found it useful to . . ."

Close your criticism by expressing confidence in the person's future progress.

"I'm sure that your mistake was simply an oversight and that it won't happen again."
"I'm confident that you'll become better and better at this."
"I know that your mistake was simply a temporary lapse that you'll easily correct."

Help people conquer habitual indecisiveness by sometimes refraining from giving advice. When you feel that people are asking you for advice just so that they can avoid making decisions and can blame you if the advice doesn't work out, determine first whether they genuinely want your advice.

"Are you asking me to tell you what to do?"
"I hear you asking me to tell you what to do."
"Do you want to know what I would do, or do you want to avoid forming your own decision?"

6

Asserting Your Rights
and
Expressing Your Feelings

People who know how to assert their rights and express their feelings *productively* are able to stand up for themselves without putting down others. They know how to claim their rights without violating other people's rights, how to demand respect without being disrespectful to others.

Although it is difficult for many people to walk the line between assertiveness and aggression, it is possible to be assertive without attacking others. You'll need first to understand the distinction between assertiveness and aggression.

People who are assertive believe that both they *and* others deserve respect. They desire to achieve their goals while realizing that other people are also important and have feelings and goals. In short, assertive people acknowledge that they are important while realizing equally well that the universe doesn't revolve around them but contains other people who also have desires and needs and rights.

In This Section

In this section you'll learn to express your principles and preferences, say "no" to those who may be trying to manipulate you, avoid dogmatism and condemnation, and express forgiveness. With carefully chosen language, you can be both tactful *and* assertive.

Dare to hold fast to your principles. Say "no" to those who expect you complacently to accept the status quo.

"No!"
"I disagree! I believe that . . ."
"No, thank you; I don't care to. I've never done that and don't want to start."
"I can't do that."
"I make it a habit never to . . ."
"I make it a habit always to . . ."
"As a matter of principle, I . . ."

When you have a strong opinion, express it as your preference rather than as a black-and-white statement of what is "bad" or "good," "right" or "wrong," or some other value judgment (as in, "This is right,"

"This is wrong," "I'm right," "This is better than that").

"I dislike . . ."
"I like . . ."
"I really don't like that!"
"I prefer . . ."

When you feel that someone is using screams and insults to try to get you to change your mind, *say so* rather than become angry and antagonistic. That practice immediately clarifies the real source of the anger and moves the argument away from name-calling and toward addressing the real issues.

"I guess you'd like me to change what I just said."
"I really believe in what I said, and I'm not going to agree with you just to get you to like me. I'm sorry, but you'll have to deal with your own feelings about it."
"You're upset about my opinions on this subject."
"You mean you disagree with what I said."
"You mean you don't like . . ."

If you feel that people often ignore your interests and desires, state your preferences clearly. You may not always be able to change their decisions, but you will make your friends and associates aware that you have certain preferences and that you want their respect when decisions are being made.

"I'd like . . ."
"I want . . ."
"I'd prefer . . ."

Instead of letting disagreements or other unfinished business between you and others go unresolved, simply *say* that there is something on your mind.

"I've been concerned about . . . for some time."
"I've been wanting to talk to you about . . ."
"Something has been bothering me for some time now, and I'd like to get it off my chest."
"I've been worried about you."

When you feel angry with someone, express your anger as *your own feelings*, not as condemnations of the person with whom you are angry (as in, "You're a jerk," or, "You're stupid"). Describe *how* you feel, not *what* the other person "is" or "is not" or "should" or "shouldn't" be.

"I'm concerned about . . ."
"I'm mad!"
"I am *very* angry."
"I *strongly* disagree with you."
"I'm becoming very mad."
"I get damned mad when you say [or "do"] that."

"I'm very distressed by this whole thing."
"I'm boiling mad!"
"I am extremely upset!"

When someone is angry with you and begins yelling at you, simply acknowledge the person's anger. State what you believe your antagonist is feeling rather than become angry yourself. Remember that all people are ultimately the authors of their own feelings—no one can "make" someone else angry.

"I'm sorry that you're upset; can I do anything to help you feel better?"
"You're getting upset, and you feel that I shouldn't have done what I did."

When you are bothered by someone's actions, state clearly what you are angry about.

"When you [criticize me in front of your friends], I feel [embarrassment]."
"When you [ridicule other people's religious beliefs], I feel [anger]."

When you feel that someone is being inconsiderate of your feelings or otherwise abusing you, tell the person how you feel about that treatment (or, if necessary, tell the person to stop) as calmly as possible. Asserting your right to be respected as a person is almost always much less stressful than harboring resentment toward the perpetrator or outrightly insulting the perpetrator, and you may often gain respect for having done so.

> "I feel very much annoyed by what you're doing."
>
> "I don't appreciate your comments."
>
> "Please talk to me nicely."
>
> "I'd appreciate better treatment."
>
> "You have no right to say [or "do"] that!"
>
> "This is unsatisfactory."
>
> "This is not what I paid for."
>
> "I don't think I've been treated fairly."
>
> "Even though I feel your criticism is accurate, I feel that you're being somewhat harsh in your tone, and I don't think that's necessary. (If you would also find something to compliment me on occasionally, the criticisms might be easier for me to accept.)"

When people are treating you inconsiderately, try to explain why it's in their best interest to treat you differently. The idea here is *not* to threaten people but to let them know how their actions might have consequences they have overlooked.

> "I don't think that it's in your best interest to . . . because . . ."
>
> "If you do that, I think that there may be a number of consequences you'll not like, such as . . ."

Be quick to accept sincere apologies and show that you don't hold grudges.

"Relax, I won't hold it against you."

"That's okay; I still like you."

"I can understand how it happened."

"I would probably have done the same thing."

"No problem."

"I forgive you."

"I appreciate that [the apology]."

"I'm sure you didn't mean to . . ."

"Please don't feel bad about what happened; I understand."

7

Handling Criticism
And Disagreement

One of the most difficult things for people to do is to accept criticism and disagreement without becoming upset or defensive. Most people see criticism and disagreement as threats or challenges to their worth, because they interpret them from a purely negative point of view.

To help combat defensive responses to criticism, you need to understand that not all criticism is accurate, and that no criticism proves that you as a person are fundamentally defective. You need further to understand that an effective way to deal with criticism is to determine whether it is accurate and then to respond accordingly. If it is inaccurate, you calmly but assertively explain why you believe it is unjustified. If it is accurate, you accept it and try to learn from it, always remembering that criticism of your conduct doesn't mean that *you* are unworthy.

In This Section

In this section you'll find carefully worded expressions that will enable you to respond to criticism assertively—from the point of view of someone who has enough self-esteem to accept and even profit from others' criticisms without feeling threatened. You'll find expressions that will enable you freely to admit any mistakes you have made, "own up" to being imperfect, acknowledge whatever is correct in others' criticisms of your actions, and accept criticism graciously.

You'll also learn expressions that will enable you to respond appropriately to those who disagree with you. Note that to respond appropriately you need to realize that it is possible for people to disagree without anyone's being guilty of anything. Since people approach situations with vastly different experiences, teachings, and traditions, disagreement is inevitable. What isn't inevitable, however, is your response to disagreement. It is your choice whether you see in disagreement a reason to condemn either yourself or others.

To help you cope with disagreement creatively, you need expressions that emphasize points of agreement even within disagreements, paraphrase important statements, call for defining key terms, request evidence for conclusions, make it easier for people to moderate their positions, and show your sensitivity to others' feelings.

You'll find that you are more likely to avoid confrontations and to resolve differences peaceably by habitually using the expressions in this section. Indeed, knowing what phrases to use to defuse arguments and handle criticisms will help make you a true winner: not simply one who can "win" an argument but one who, more important, can win a friend!

Accept reasonable criticism and good advice graciously. Where possible, sincerely praise people for correcting you.

"Thanks for telling me that."
"I appreciate your advice because now I'll be better able to . . ."
"It takes class to offer criticism without upsetting people, and you have class."
"Thanks, I can use that."
"Thanks, I'll try that."

Freely acknowledge the correctness of others, even when it shows that you were incorrect.

"You're right. I was wrong."
"You've changed my opinion."
"You've persuaded me to change my position."

Show people that you willingly and promptly admit mistakes.

"I goofed."
"I made a mistake."
"I did it."

Show people that you make no claim to being perfect.

"I must admit that . . ."
"In all honesty . . ."
"I'll be the first to acknowledge my limitations in
    this matter."

Before you respond to people's criticisms or claims,
hear them out without interrupting them and *thank*
them for having the courage to express their thoughts.
This technique encourages people generally to feel
freer to express their ideas around you.

It is, therefore, especially effective if you are a
supervisor or other person who has authority over
those who disagree with you.

"I want to thank you for having enough courage
    to disagree with me."
"Whatever our differences, I respect you for
    speaking your mind."
"I appreciate your having enough interest in this
    issue to bring up those objections."
"I admire people who can argue persuasively."
"You've made a persuasive argument, and I
    appreciate that. (Here's how I feel about this
    matter: . . .)"

Try to find at least one thing you can agree on about
someone's criticism or claim before you attempt to
defend yourself against the criticism or to attack the
claim.

"You are correct in saying that I . . . Let me just
point out also that . . ."

"There is a lot of truth in what you're saying. It
may also be helpful to consider that . . ."

To help resolve major points of disagreement, focus
first on points of *agreement*.

"I think we both have the same concerns—our
only disagreements are with how to approach
the problem."

"I think we can both agree that . . ."

"I think we agree . . ."

"Would you agree that . . . ?"

"We both feel strongly about . . ."

"We both believe that . . ."

"In some ways our positions are alike. For
example, . . ."

"I am somewhat like you because . . ."

Whenever there is a chance that you may sound as if
you are disagreeing with something that you in fact
are not disagreeing with, say so.

"Please understand that this is in no way a
disagreement with what you said."

"This is not intended to mean that I disagree
with your decision."

"This does not mean that I don't appreciate what
you've done."

Make sure to clarify major points of disagreement by restating what you understand the other person to be saying.

> "Am I correct in taking you to mean . . . ?"
> "I understand you to be saying that . . ."
> "You are saying that . . ."
> "If I take your point of view, . . ."

Make sure to clarify major points of disagreement by defining crucial terms.

> "Let's define our terms."
> "Let's be sure that we're talking about the same thing."
> "The term you're using is ambiguous, since it might mean (a) . . . or (b) . . . , depending on the context."*

Strive to identify and eliminate the minor issues in an argument and bring out the arguer's main complaint or contention.

> "What is your *main* gripe?"
> "I think my main concern is that . . ."
> "Does this bother you the most, or is it something else that really concerns you?"

---

*Naturally, you'd use that sentence only if some term is ambiguous.

Show that you want to resolve differences in arguments by encouraging people to clarify their positions and helping them to understand your position.

"On what points do we see eye to eye?"
"Would you like me to clarify any aspect of my position?"
"Could you describe specifically any aspects of my position that strike you as inflexible or unreasonable?"
"Can you think of a more constructive approach to our disagreement?"
"Let's try to come up with some answers that will help both of us."

If you must interrupt someone, give some sign of courteousness.

"Excuse me."
"I'm sorry for interrupting you; I just wanted to clarify . . ."

Ask others to support their claims with evidence.

"Can you give me some examples?"
"Can you think of how your principle would work, or be applied, in practice?"

Ask for evidence when people make unsupported claims.

"Where did you hear that?"
"According to whom?"
"On what evidence are you basing that
   judgment?"

Help others to clarify any of their claims that are based
solely on what "they say."

"Who are 'they'?"
"What evidence do 'they' have?"

Help others to revise any of their dogmatic and unqual-
ified judgments (e.g., "This is good"; "This is bad";
"This is worse"; "This is better"; "This is wrong";
"*All* people do it"; "*Everyone* knows that . . ."; "It
happens *every* time"; "Those people *never* . . .";
"There are too many . . ."; "This is too much . . .").

"You mean you feel that it's bad *for you*."
"You mean that *in your opinion* this is worse."
"How do you know?"
"According to whom?"
"Compared to what?"
"Perhaps you mean 'many' instead of 'all.' "
"Perhaps you mean 'often' instead of 'always.' "
"Perhaps you mean 'seldom' instead of
   'never.' "
"Perhaps you mean 'very few' instead of
   'none.' "

Admit when you are uncertain about your claims. This
practice keeps you from appearing inflexible and dog-

matic and makes the other person feel freer to express contrary opinions.

"I may be mistaken, but . . ."
"If I am mistaken, and I certainly have been before, I want to be corrected."
"You may be perfectly in the right, but I personally prefer . . ."

Spice your claims with examples.

"For example, . . ."
"To illustrate my point, . . ."

If you have made any claims or assertions that you think may have offended people, promptly let them know that your intent was not to offend them.

"I didn't mean to say anything offensive, and I want you to know that your feelings matter more to me than what we are discussing."
"Please realize that I'd never intentionally hurt your feelings, which are more important to me than the issues we are now discussing."
"I hope my remarks haven't offended you; if they have, please accept my apologies—I sometimes get carried away, but I don't intend to hurt anyone."

If someone has made a statement that is proved incorrect, give the person some ways to save face; don't rub it in.

"Please think nothing of accepting that misconception—I used to believe it myself."

"You're not alone in having thought that; nearly everyone believes it."

"I probably would have believed the same thing had I not read/seen . . ."

"You probably didn't have access to all the relevant facts."

"I wish I had a dollar for every time *I* accepted a belief that turned out to be false."

If an argument becomes heated, and it is clear that neither side is going to accomplish anything, stop and perhaps agree to delay further arguing until tempers cool down.

"Please stop, since we are both becoming too emotional to talk about these matters rationally."

"Please, let's agree to talk about this when we're calmer."

When someone continues to argue after you feel that you have fairly and genuinely addressed that person's requests or criticisms, it is better simply to acknowledge the person's remarks than to get into another argument.

"I hear you."

"Got you."

"You're entitled to your opinion."

"You've already made yourself clear on this matter."

Always be open to compromise where friendship is concerned.

"Suppose we try to agree at least that . . ."
"Can we make some arrangement that will satisfy both of us?"
"Can we compromise?"
"I'm willing to compromise."

Take the opportunity to apologize whenever there is the least chance that ill will could set in.

"I want to apologize for . . ."
"I forgot to . . . ; I'm sorry."

If an argument was particularly heated, make sure to leave the arguer with an assurance that you do not want the argument to affect your relationship.

"Please let's not allow this disagreement to hurt a friendship we deeply value."
"I value our relationship too much to let this disagreement ruin it—I'm confident that we both agree on that."
"You mean too much to me for me to allow this disagreement to stand between us."

Show people that you care about their feelings by promptly acknowledging whenever you have been inconsiderate, insensitive, rude, or discourteous.

> "That was insensitive [or "rude" or "discourteous"] of me. I'm sorry."

Try as much as you can to emphasize something positive about the person to whom you apologize.

> "I misjudged you—you handled [whatever the task was] like a pro, and I apologize for thinking otherwise."
> "I owe you an apology for taking advantage of your habitual kindness."
> "Your information is practically always reliable; I apologize for doubting you."

8

Getting Things Done

Getting things done depends not only on your efficiency but also on your ability to persuade and direct others. For we are all interdependent: friends need to gain emotional support; supervisors need to direct their workers; family members need to help one another; and so on. Yet, many supervisors belittle and alienate their workers; many friends risk appearing inconsiderate to one another; and many family members feel manipulated by the others. An important cause of those frictions and tensions is the inconsiderate and inept use of language, in which people not only fail to express respect and gratitude but neglect to reveal precisely what they want. Much harm is caused by people who use language that is imprecise and misleading, that obscures rather than clarifies people's intentions and expectations.

To manage your time well, you'll need other people's cooperation. To achieve their cooperation, you'll need language that precisely expresses your expectations and reflects your gratitude for help.

In This Section

In this section you'll find phrases and sentences that will help you to establish deadlines and priorities, to clarify intentions, to gain precise information, to ask for advice, to delegate authority, and to save time. By habitually using these expressions, you'll promote cooperation and accomplish more in less time.

Show people that you care about doing well at your tasks by encouraging others to give you advice for improvement. Their advice not only will help you but also will raise the self-esteem of the one who gives the advice. Your request for their advice tells them that you value their opinions.

"How am I doing?"
"How can I do better at this task?"
"Is there any way I might improve my
    performance?"
"What could I have done differently?"
"If you were I, what would you have done?"
"Please let me benefit from your valuable
    experience by explaining how I might improve
    on this."

Establish definite deadlines for accomplishing important tasks.

"By [date/time], you'll . . ."
"By [date/time], we'll . . ."

When you must rely on others to get things done, prompt them to establish definite work times by starting with "When . . . ?" questions. Asking "Can I . . . ?" or "Will you . . . ?" makes it too easy for them to answer "No!"

"When is a good day for us to . . . ?"
"When shall I . . . ?"
"When do you want me to . . . ?"
"When do you want to . . . ?"

Show flexibility and patience. Try to use language that does not make others feel as though you are rushing them. Often people will do better jobs when they don't feel rushed. Further, if you make it a habit usually not to rush people, they will be more willing to help you out on those few occasions you do need something done quickly.

"Please take your time."
"There's no need to rush on my account."
"It's no hurry—please do it when you have more time."
"I won't ask you to rush very often; this time,

though, I really could use your speed and
efficiency to get this done by [time/date]."

Delegate wisely, establishing clearly who is responsible for which important tasks.

"Who'll be responsible for that?"
"It would be a big help to me if you would
. . ."
"I know you're good at . . . , so I'd like you to
do this."
"Could you give me a hand?"*

Establish priorities, completing the most pressing matters first, by finding out by what date something must be completed.

"What's the latest you'd like to have this?"

Save time and increase efficiency by eliminating unnecessary work.

"Is this necessary?"
"Could we shorten this by eliminating . . . ?"

---

*People will respond positively to your requests *especially* when you preface them with good reasons. For example, if your back is bothering you or you have an important meeting or some other legitimate time-taker, say so. However, if you're vague about your reasons for making the requests, as when you say that you "need to do something else" or you're simply "too busy," you may want to be more specific.

Make minor everyday decisions quickly. This practice prevents procrastination and saves time that can be spent on more important work.

> "Yes, that's fine; thank you."
> "No, I'm not interested, thank you."
> "Thanks, but I am *quite* certain that I am not interested."*

When you don't have time for small talk with unexpected visitors or telephone callers, promptly but politely let them know about your schedule.

> "Unfortunately, I'll need to leave within ___ minutes to meet my schedule."
> "To be on time, I'll have to leave in a few minutes/seconds."

When someone asks whether you "have a minute," clarify how limited your time is.

> "Can we really do it in a minute?"
> "I have ___ minutes now, but if it takes longer, we'll have to continue it later."

When you are asked to make quick decisions that require careful thought, delay firm replies unless promptness is necessary. This practice removes much

---

*That sentence is especially useful when you are confronted by stubborn salespeople or telephone solicitors.

unnecessary stress and shows others that you want your decisions to be wise.

> "If you don't need this answer right away, I'd like to give it some additional thought before I give you a definite answer."
> "Today is inconvenient. [Another date] would be much better."
> "Let me think about it."
> "I'd like to think about that. I'll get back to you."
> "I'll let you know."
> "I'll call you back as soon as I can."
> "This sounds important, so I don't want to make a snappy decision. I'll get back to you."
> "I may be interested, but I'll need some more time to think about it."
> "Since I make it a habit never to rush into these matters, I need some more time."

When people want you to complete a task in less time than you believe you'll need, first let them know how much time (as precisely as possible) you'll need. This initial response is almost always superior to replying, "I can't do it."

> "I appreciate your need for promptness; however, I'll need another [amount of additional time] to do a competent job."
> "That sounds important, and in all honesty I believe I can only do it if I have [amount of

additional time] to produce the kind of results that you and I would prefer.''

Be sure that you are prepared to accept full responsibility for the commitments you make, and whenever possible avoid making promises on behalf of others.

''I make it a practice not to make commitments others must honor.''

''Since I don't know what her plans are for that day, I can't assure you that she will be available.''

''You'll need to talk to him, since you're talking about his time.''

Distinguish between your intentions and your promises.

''I'll try my best to complete the project by [date], but I can't promise you that I'll be able to.''

''Please understand that, while I fully intend to do this for you, my other duties—including . . .—often must take precedence; so I can't guarantee that I'll get it done.''

Make sure that those to whom you delegate tasks are clear about their assignments and that they realize that you are not abandoning them.

"Specifically, what are you trying to accomplish?"

"Can you please specify the steps you'll take to achieve the primary goals?"

"Can you tell me how and when you'll keep me posted on your progress?"

"In what form will you express your final results?"

"When do you think you'll complete your assignment?"

"How much authority do you need?"

"What, if anything, will you need from me?"

To assure that people will remember your instructions to them, encourage them to repeat what you have said. Be sure, however, to ask in such a way that you don't appear to be questioning their competence or intelligence.

"Can you repeat what I said, so that I'll be sure I made myself clear?"

When you have important ideas that you want others to understand clearly, give people the opportunity to ask you questions. When you ask for questions, try to show sincerity and avoid sounding mechanical.

"Are there any questions? I'll be happy to clarify or elaborate."

"Please feel free to ask me questions, which I enjoy answering."

"Am I making myself clear?"
"Am I painting a clear picture of this?"
"Does what I'm saying sound right to you?"
"Are you able to get a handle on this?"
"Do you understand what I'm trying to
  communicate?"

When you are asked an important question whose answer you are in doubt about, be willing to show that doubt rather than pretend to be perfect. Ultimately, you'll feel better if you're honest, and people will respect you for your honest expression of your limitations.

"I'm not sure."
"I don't know."

To learn, always ask for additional information rather than try to appear perfect. In the process, you show that you care about learning and respect other people's knowledge.

"I have some questions I'd like to ask you."
"Since I know you are well educated in these
  matters, could you explain . . . ?"

When you want the most detailed information, start a question with "what" or "how." In contrast, to ask, "Do you know anything about . . . ?" or "Do you have any . . . ?" often leads only to a "no" reply, or no further than a "yes."

"What can you tell me about . . . ?"
"How many . . . do you have?"
"How would you suggest that I [do
    something]?"

When you want to make difficult requests of people,
first show that you care enough about people to notice
their particular circumstance.

"You look as if you're having a pretty rough
    day."
"You look as if you've been working very
    hard."
"You look as if you're quite busy."
"I realize that you're busy, but could you
    . . . ?"

To help accomplish difficult tasks effectively and effi-
ciently, become aware of those persons who have wis-
dom and experience you lack, and ask for their help.

"Let's pool our resources."
"Since each of us has a great deal of experience,
    we can profit from working together."
"I'd deeply appreciate our combining our
    talents."

When you need people's advice or assistance, first
build up their confidence in their ability to help you.
Use sincere praise of their expertise, and try to make

them feel that their opinions are valuable. People will want to help you if they know that they're appreciated.

> "I know that you're an authority on this subject."
>
> "I was told that if anyone could help, it would be you."
>
> "I've always been able to make good use of your suggestions in the past; so I hope you might have the time to give me some advice in this matter, too."
>
> "I value your expertise."
>
> "I like asking you for your opinions because I know that they're based on sound reasoning and much experience."

When you ask for favors, try to offer something in return. It is all too easy thoughtlessly to expect favors from friends and associates without ever making an effort to reciprocate in some way, however small.

> "If you . . . , I'll . . ."

When you make a request or broach a sensitive subject, show courtesy and avoid acting as though the person is obligated to serve you or answer you.

> "I'd appreciate it if you would . . ."
>
> "May I ask . . . ?"
>
> "Would it be convenient for you [or "me"] to . . . ?"

"Is this a good time?"
"When [or "what"] is best for you?"
"I hope I haven't come [or "called"] at a bad
  time."
"May I . . . ?"
"I will respect your wishes."
"Will this be okay with you?"
"Please . . ."

When you are confused about what someone is telling
you, sacrifice any desire to "look like you know it
all" for a willingness to understand fully.

"I don't understand; please enlighten me."
"I don't think I follow you."
"I'm not sure I understand."

To assure that you have understood someone else's
instructions, restate what you think you have heard,
giving the other person the opportunity to correct you
if you believe your understanding is inaccurate or in-
complete.

"Did you say . . . ?"

Whenever you haven't been paying attention, admit it
rather than risk not knowing what was said.

"I'm sorry. I was daydreaming. Could you
  repeat that?"

Acknowledge others' help, and try also to express *how* it helped you.

"I took your advice, and it worked."

"I used your suggestion; it was very helpful."

"Your advice was a great help."

"You've relieved me of a lot of worry."

"Thanks for talking to me about that; I feel a lot better now."

"You've solved my problem."

Conclusion

Success means keeping old friends, turning strangers into friends, maintaining a caring family, and being a respected boss and an admired worker. If you are to live successfully, you need to respect others and yourself. And you need to use language that expresses respect. The more you use Success Phrases, the better you'll get along with others and the more respect you'll have for yourself.

Your Success Phrases will distinguish you as a person who values others as well as yourself. They will often be the first impressions—and the last impressions. If you make them a part of you, you'll never be at a loss for words . . . or friends.

By the year 2000, 2 out of 3 Americans could be illiterate.

It's true.

Today, 75 million adults... about one American in three, can't read adequately. And by the year 2000, U.S. News & World Report envisions an America with a literacy rate of only 30%.

Before that America comes to be, you can stop it... by joining the fight against illiteracy today.

Call the Coalition for Literacy at toll-free **1-800-228-8813** and volunteer.

Volunteer Against Illiteracy. The only degree you need is a degree of caring.

Ad Council Coalition for Literacy

Warner Books is proud to be an active supporter of the Coalition for Literacy.